The Crude, Unpleasant Age of Pirates

THE DISGUSTING DETAILS ABOUT THE LIFE OF PIRATES

by Christopher Forest

raintree

a Capstone company — publishers for children

Raintree is an imprint of Capstone Global Library Limited, a company incorporated in England and Wales having its registered office at 264 Banbury Road, Oxford, OX2 7DY – Registered company number: 6695582

www.raintree.co.uk
myorders@raintree.co.uk

Edited by Katy Kudela
Designed by Álison Thiele and Gene Bentdahl
Picture research by Wanda Winch
Production by Eric Manske

ISBN 978 1 4747 1962 9
19 18 17 16 15
10 9 8 7 6 5 4 3 2 1

British Library Cataloguing in Publication Data
A full catalogue record for this book is available from the British Library.

Photo Credits
akg-images: Museum der Bildenden Künste, 9; Alamy: Lebrecht Music and Arts Photo Library, 14, Paris Pierce, 10; The Bridgeman Art Library: ©Look and Learn/Private Collection/Peter Jackson, 18, ©Look and Learn/Private Collection/Ron Embleton, 11 (right), 27, Peter Newark Historical Pictures/Private Collection, 16, Peter Newark Historical Pictures/Private Collection/C.T. Howard, 21, Private Collection/A.D. McClintock, 23, Private Collection/Jean Leon Jerome Ferris, 28; iStockphoto: NoDerog, 4 (br), Stanislav Pobytov, 4 (tl); ©National Maritime Museum, Greenwich, London, 13; Nova Development Corporation, 5 (all); Rick Reeves, Tampa, FL: cover, 7, 24: Shutterstock: akva, 14, 21 (old notebook), Andreas Meyer, 4 (bl), Baloncici, 12, freelanceartist, grunge paper design element throughout, M.i.k.e., 8, Myotis, 20, Robb Williams, 4 (tr), Turi Tamas, banner design element throughout; www.thefruitofherhands.com/Jill Howard, 15

Primary source bibliography
Pages 14 and 21—as published in *The Buccaneers of America* by A. O. Exquemelin, Henry Powell, and Basil Ringrose (New York: The MacMillan Company, 1911).

We would like to thank Charles R. Ewen, PhD, for his invaluable help in the preparation of this book.

Every effort has been made to contact copyright holders of material reproduced in this book. Any omissions will be rectified in subsequent printings if notice is given to the publisher.

All the internet addresses (URLs) given in this book were valid at the time of going to press. However, due to the dynamic nature of the internet, some addresses may have changed, or sites may have changed or ceased to exist since publication. While the author and publisher regret any inconvenience this may cause readers, no responsibility for any such changes can be accepted by either the author or the publisher.

Printed and bound in China.

CONTENTS

THE GOLDEN AGE OF PIRATES

1690–1725

KEY

KEY
- ● CITY
- • • • • TRADE ROUTE

```
0          600 MILES
0          965 KM
```

N
W ← → E
S

1689
William Kidd earns the name of pirate; the naming of Kidd as a pirate helps usher in the Golden Age of Pirates.

PAGE 20

1693
An earthquake destroys the city of Port Royal in Jamaica; this city was a popular pirate hideout.

PIRATE CHAIN OF COMMAND

CAPTAIN elected by pirate crew to command the ship

FIRST MATE helped the captain run the ship

QUARTERMASTER handled supplies, rations and helped keep order on the ship

PILOT kept the ship on course

SAILOR general crew member

1700
Jolly Roger flags become common on pirate ships.

1701
England's government takes William Kidd to court for charges of piracy; Kidd is put to death.

1702–1713
Queen Anne's War breaks out between France and England; at the end of the war sailors are out of work and some become pirates.

PAGE 20

1714
New Providence in the Bahamas becomes a pirate hideout.

CAPTAIN BARTHOLOMEW ROBERTS

"No, a merry life and a short one shall be my motto."

as quoted in *Raiders and Rebels: The Golden Age of Piracy,* by Frank Sherry

PAGE 19

1716
Edward Teach joins a pirate crew; Teach later becomes known as Captain Blackbeard.

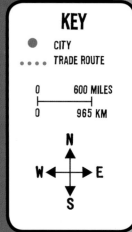

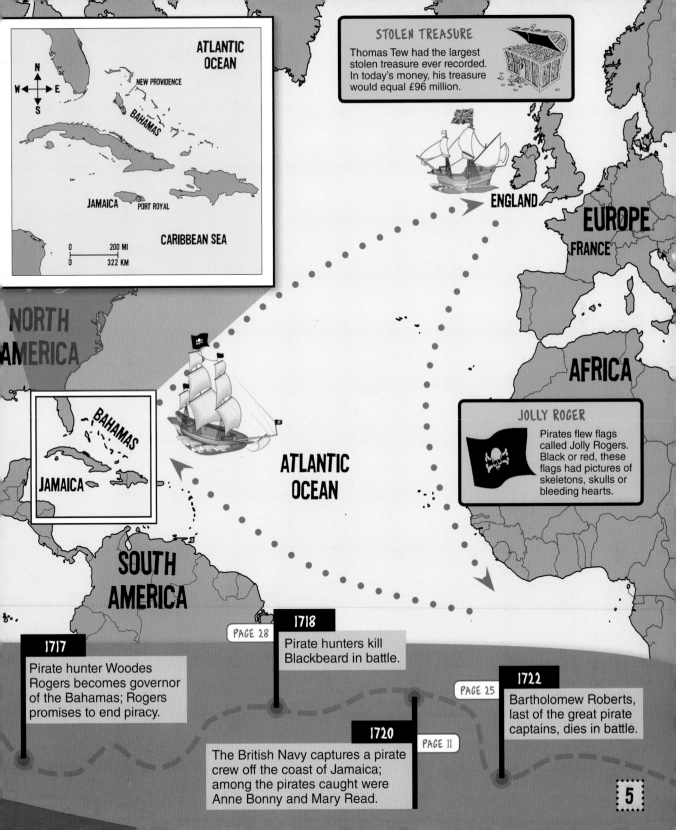

ATLANTIC OCEAN

NEW PROVIDENCE

BAHAMAS

JAMAICA   PORT ROYAL

CARIBBEAN SEA

0   200 MI
0   322 KM

STOLEN TREASURE

Thomas Tew had the largest stolen treasure ever recorded. In today's money, his treasure would equal £96 million.

ENGLAND

EUROPE

FRANCE

NORTH AMERICA

BAHAMAS

JAMAICA

ATLANTIC OCEAN

SOUTH AMERICA

AFRICA

JOLLY ROGER

Pirates flew flags called Jolly Rogers. Black or red, these flags had pictures of skeletons, skulls or bleeding hearts.

1717

Pirate hunter Woodes Rogers becomes governor of the Bahamas; Rogers promises to end piracy.

PAGE 28

1718

Pirate hunters kill Blackbeard in battle.

1720

PAGE 11

The British Navy captures a pirate crew off the coast of Jamaica; among the pirates caught were Anne Bonny and Mary Read.

PAGE 25

1722

Bartholomew Roberts, last of the great pirate captains, dies in battle.

A DEADLY CAREER

"Ahoy there, mate," orders a large man holding a sword. "To your post!" The smell of saltwater spray and seaweed fills the air as the large pirate ship readies to sail. Crowded onto the ship is a crew of dirty, sweaty men.

Each man moves about with a job to do. Some crew members struggle to pull up the ship's sails. Others blister their hands loosening ropes. Below the main deck, men move about in the dark. They stack barrels of food and water. As they work, rats scurry across the damp floor. Shouts fill the air as the ship's anchor lifts from the water. Moments later, the ship and its crew sail off on another treasure hunt.

For nearly 40 years, pirates ruled the seas. Often, pirates looked no different from the other people of their time. But make no mistake. These foul sailors certainly acted differently. Pirates made a living attacking ships, killing crews and stealing treasure. If pirates were lucky, they lived long enough to spend their money. Unlucky pirates died at sea.

A pirate had to watch his back. Even his shipmates could turn on him.

Danger filled pirates' lives. They lost limbs in battle and suffered fatal wounds. They also endured painful and deadly diseases. But weather was the greatest danger. Storms at sea damaged ships and killed crews. A pirate's life was crude and unpleasant. Still, their rough life often paid off with stolen treasure.

LIFE AT SEA

Hundreds of pirates were often packed onto a single ship. It didn't take long before foul smells filled the air. These men shared food, beds and toilets. The few items they brought with them were kept in common chests shared by others.

No matter how watertight the ship, water filled the lower deck. Pirates bailed the water out as fast as they could. Still, they could not rid the ship of its foul sewer smell. The food storage decks were a bit drier. But these decks had problems too. In these dark areas, barrels and sacks of food housed worms, spiders and rats.

Captains had private quarters, but the crew's living space was tight. Pirates slept anywhere they could find. Some chose a sack of food as a sleeping spot. Others found a dry place on the rough wooden floor. Fires were not allowed below deck, so pirates spent many cold, damp nights trying to keep warm. During hot weather, the stench of  sweat, sewage and salt water filled the ship.

On a pirate ship, sleeping on the top deck meant fresh air.

FOUL FACT

To rid their ships of rats, pirates went hunting for the pests. A Spanish crew reported finding nearly 4,000 rats.

To make conditions even worse, pirates weren't alone below deck. Hundreds of rodents crawled over the sleeping men. Infections from rat bites sent many pirates to an early grave.

A FOUL CREW

After weeks at sea, pirates looked as foul as they smelt. Pirates had dirty hair and rotten, yellow teeth. On a pirate ship, brushing teeth and bathing rarely happened. Freshwater was saved for cooking and drinking.

Sweaty, dirty men added to the disgusting stench. Most pirates only came aboard a ship with the clothes they were wearing. These clothes quickly became torn and covered in bloodstains and sweat. Washing the clothes helped, but pirates often only washed their shirts. A pirate's best chance of getting new clothes was to steal them from someone on another ship.

Picture the comfortable toilet in your house. With one flush, waste disappears. Now picture a wooden board with some holes. That's what pirates called a toilet. Most pirates relieved themselves through a simple hole in a plank at the back of the ship. A pirate had to pick the right time for his toilet break. When the waves were rough, their waste sometimes flew back onto the ship and other pirates. Yuck, look out below!

FOUL FACT

Not all pirates were men. Anne Bonny and Mary Read dressed as men when they served aboard pirate ships.

Pirates' foul reputations matched the living quarters aboard their ships.

POOR DIET

A pirate's diet was far from fine dining. The men making meals on pirate ships were not trained cooks. These men were often crew members who had lost an arm or a leg in battle. They had no cooking skills and few supplies.

On a cramped ship, cooks did their best to feed hundreds of hungry men. Some ships had small kitchens. Other ships had no kitchens at all. Cooks made meals in large kettles over fires. On windy days, pirates did no cooking. One spark from a cook's fire could burn down the whole ship.

Before setting sail, pirates stocked up on vegetables and meat. But keeping food fresh was no easy task. Fresh food only lasted a few weeks. To help the food last longer, cooks poured salt over it. As time went on, the food rotted. Cooks then used spices to mask the bad taste and served the rotten food anyway.

Wooden barrels kept food dry.

Pirates raided towns for food and other supplies.

No food in sight

For these first took the leather, and sliced it in pieces. Then did they beat it between two stones, and rub it, often dipping it in the water of the river, to render it by these means supple and tender. Lastly, they scraped off the hair, and roasted or broiled it upon the fire.

Above quotation is based on the writing of Alexandre Olivier Exquemelin, as published in The Buccaneers of America, 1911.

Pirate ships sailed for weeks and months at a time. Their supplies did not last a whole voyage. Out at sea, pirates had several ways to restock their ship with food. They took food from the ships and towns they attacked. Pirates stopped at islands to hunt monkeys, birds and turtles. They also fished for dolphins, tuna and sea turtles.

Pirates ate a steady diet of hardtack. Made of flour and water, these hard biscuits didn't spoil as quickly as meat. Hardtack was a simple meal for ship cooks to prepare. While hardtack was easy to keep, there were still a few problems. Hardtack quickly turned stale. Tiny bugs called weevils also found their way into these biscuits. But hungry pirates didn't care. They ate the hardtack, bugs and all.

Occasionally, pirates had no food to eat. Cooks then had to make do with whatever they could find. When supplies were low, cooks used fish bones, animal bones and even rats to make a nasty batch of bone soup.

HARDTACK

ARMED FOR BATTLE

Pirate ships carried deadly weapons. A single pirate ship often carried up to 40 cannon. Pirates had to be skilled when firing cannon. Misfires could give pirates frightful burns and even take an arm or a leg off.

Fear was a pirate crew's best weapon. A raised flag or a warning shot were often enough to get another ship to surrender. When these warnings didn't work, pirate captains did not think twice about ordering an all-out attack. Some captains even ordered "no quarter". This order meant that pirates would fight to the death.

Boom! During attacks, pirates fired a **volley** onto the deck of the enemy ship. Pirates wanted to hurt the crew but not the ship. The volley sprayed glass, metal or nails across the ship's deck. Unlucky crew members were left bloody or even blinded.

Pirates fired warning shots.

volley warning shot fired from a gun or cannon

Pirates showed no mercy in battle. They would stop at nothing to get their treasure.

Painful volleys were often followed by grenades. These handmade bombs were dangerous. Once the grenade was lit, a pirate only had a matter of seconds before it blew. Pirates also threw stinkpots. They filled these clay pots with sulphur and rotten fish.

Pirates then muscled their way aboard in hand-to-hand combat. Pistols and muskets caused horrible injuries at close range. In most battles, pirates did not have much time to reload their guns. Once they had fired them, pirates used their guns as clubs to strike their enemies. They also used cutlasses in close fighting. The sharp, curved edge of these swords cut deep, causing deadly wounds.

FOUL FACT

Blackbeard carried pistols, knives and two swords with him at all times. He was one of the most feared pirates of the Golden Age.

PIRATE TREASURE

Pirates were willing to suffer disease, foul food and deadly battles for one thing: treasure! Pirates captured ships and took their prized **booty**. In a pirate's world, almost anything was treasure. Pirates sold cloth, spices and supplies for money. They even sold slaves. From anchors to rope, pirates stripped ships bare. Sometimes they even took the ship itself.

Beware! No one was safe when pirates went looking for treasure. Pirate crews sometimes held prisoners and whole towns to **ransom**. Pirates like Blackbeard showed no mercy. Stories say Blackbeard sliced off a man's finger just to get the man's diamond ring.

What did pirates do with their treasure? Few pirates, if any, buried their treasure. Most pirates sailed to hideouts. Port Royal, Jamaica and New Providence in the Bahamas were favourite stops. Pirates felt at home in these wild ports. But they soon lost their money playing cards and dice.

booty stolen goods

ransom money that is demanded before someone or something will be set free

Pirates divided their treasure once they made it to shore.

Not all gold and riches

The ship being taken, they found none in her what they thought … All the treasure they got consisted only in fifty bars of iron, a small parcel of paper, some earthen jars full of wine and other things of this kind; all of small importance.

Above quotation is based on the writing of Alexandre Olivier Exquemelin, as published in The Buccaneers of America, 1911.

BETTER NOT GET SICK!

Pirates had treasure, but what they really needed were doctors. On a pirate ship, a cook or carpenter acted as the ship's doctor. These sailors had no medical training. They were chosen because they had a knife or saw. As ship doctors, they needed these tools to cut off injured arms and legs.

During battles, pirates suffered many injuries. With little medicine or clean water, wounds became infected. Arms and legs that did not heal were **amputated**. The ship's doctor often had to cut off the limb within 24 hours of the injury. Doctors used a red-hot saw or knife to remove the limb. They hoped the heat of the knife or saw would stop the bleeding. If so, a pirate might just live. Of course, a pirate first had to make it through all the pain. There was no medicine, so pirates were awake through the entire operation.

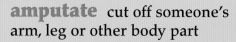

amputate cut off someone's arm, leg or other body part

On dirty ships, disease spread quickly. Dysentery and smallpox wiped out pirate crews. Many more pirates suffered from scurvy. This painful disease gave pirates loose teeth, rotten gums and bleeding under the skin. If left untreated, patients died. To stop scurvy, pirates drank ale with herbs. Later, they learnt to eat citrus fruit to prevent the disease.

On a pirate ship, many battle wounds turned deadly.

After many days at sea, tempers flared and fights broke out.

PIRATE CODES

After months at sea, pirates grew restless and often fought each other or their captain. It wasn't easy for a captain to keep order over a crew of men. Pirates were stuck together for many days. These hot, tired men often lashed out at one other.

Most pirate captains kept control through fear and harsh punishments. Pirate codes helped captains run their ships. These codes were a strict set of rules pirates had to follow.

One of the most famous set of pirate codes was created by Bartholomew "Black Bart" Roberts. This fierce captain kept a tight ship. His men could not gamble. Candles had to be put out at 8 pm each night. Pirates aboard Black Bart's ship had to follow the codes or risk injury and even death.

No matter which code, every pirate captain had one thing in mind: controlling the ship. A captain's worst fear was **mutiny**. During a mutiny, unhappy pirates tried to rid a ship of its captain and his loyal crew. Some angry crews killed their captains. Others sent their captains out to sea in small boats with no food or water.

mutiny revolt against the captain of a ship

KEEPING ORDER

Life on a pirate ship was clear-cut. Pirates who followed the rules and fought in battles were rewarded. Pirates who broke the rules faced terrible punishments.

On a pirate ship, even minor crimes had painful punishments. A pirate who took a lit candle below deck was **flogged**. The guilty pirate was only whipped once on the back. Left with a scar, the pirate would never forget this punishment.

A repeated or serious crime could lead to keelhauling. For this punishment, a ship's crew tied a pirate to a rope. They lowered him into the water and dragged him under the ship. Sharp barnacles shredded the pirate's skin. His lungs quickly filled with water. Keelhauling was almost always deadly.

What's a punishment worse than death? Being **marooned**. Angry captains marooned pirates on islands. These islands were often just sandbars, reefs or stretches of empty land with no food or freshwater. The marooned pirate was given a bottle of water or rum and a pistol loaded with a single shot. Pirates could use the pistol to end their suffering. But many marooned pirates slowly starved to death. Others were swept away by the ocean tides.

Few marooned pirates
lived to tell the tale.

flog whip someone with a special whip called the cat-o'-nine-tails

maroon leave someone behind on a deserted island

After Blackbeard was killed, British sailors hung his head from their ship's bow as a warning to other pirates.

GOLDEN AGE ENDS

During the golden age, pirates sailed the seas risking death and disease for treasure. But by the 1720s, their days were numbered. Navies around the world began to fight back against pirates.

Pirate hunters chased and captured pirates. At sea, navies attacked and destroyed pirate ships.

Captured pirates were quickly tried and hanged for their crimes. Town officials hung pirate bodies in harbours. These rotting bodies were a grim warning for pirates hoping to come ashore.

By the early 1800s, the life of pirates had changed. The pirates who once ruled the seas were now just outlaws on the run. They were no longer fierce hunters. Instead, pirates had become the hunted. Their captures and deaths brought an end to their golden age.

Even the feared pirate Blackbeard was killed by pirate hunters.

GLOSSARY

amputate cut off someone's arm, leg or other body part, usually because the part is damaged

booty stolen goods

deck floor of a boat or a ship

flog whip someone with a special whip called a cat-o'-nine-tails

maroon leave someone behind on a deserted island

mutiny revolt against the captain of a ship

ransom money that is demanded before someone or something will be set free

volley warning shot fired from a gun or cannon

READ MORE

Pirates (Project X), Jane Penrose (Oxford University Press)

Pirate Treasure (Treasure Hunters), Nick Hunter (Raintree, 2013)

Pirate's Handbook, Sam Taplin (Usborne Publishing Ltd, 2014)

WEBSITES

www.rmg.co.uk/explore/sea-and-ships/facts/ships-and-seafarers/pirates
Find out more about famous pirates through history on the National Maritime Museum's website.

www.the-pirate-ship.com/index.html
Discover facts about famous pirates, pirate's code and more.

INDEX